Abyssinian kittens owned by Marti Higgins.

ABYSSINIANS
KW-223

CONTENTS

ACKNOWLEDGMENTS

My thanks to Georgia Morgan, President of The International Cat Association, for supplying me with the four color standards of the Abyssinian Cat, and to Evelyn Mague for the Somali standards.

Thank you all, and I hope you enjoy my book.

Ruth Cooke-Zimmermann

DEDICATION

I dedicate this book to all of the special people who are fortunate enough to live with and love the most exquisite, loving, and beautiful of cats—the Abyssinian.

Photographers: *Ruth Cooke-Zimmermann, Donna Coss, JAL Duncan, Isabelle Francais, Dawn Grubb, Marti Higgins, Dorothy Holby, Juell Studio, Lewis Fineman, Maja Lohrengel, Darrell Newkirk, Ray Paulsen, Robert Pearcy, Gale Taylor, Thompson Photographics, Sheila Warmack.*

Title page: Gr. Ch. Izod's All That Jazz, a beautiful Abyssinian owned by Marti Higgins.

1996 Edition

9 8 7 6 5 4 3 2 1   95 789

Distributed in the UNITED STATES to the Pet Trade by T.F.H. Publications, Inc., One T.F.H. Plaza, Neptune City, NJ 07753; distributed in the UNITED STATES to the Bookstore and Library Trade by National Book Network, Inc. 4720 Boston Way, Lanham MD 20706; in CANADA to the Pet Trade by H & L Pet Supplies Inc., 27 Kingston Crescent, Kitchener, Ontario N2B 2T6; Rolf C. Hagen Inc., 3225 Sartelon St. Laurent-Montreal Quebec H4R 1E8; in CANADA to the Book Trade by Vanwell Publishing Ltd., 1 Northrup Crescent, St. Catharines, Ontario L2M 6P5 ; in ENGLAND by T.F.H. Publications, PO Box 15, Waterlooville PO7 6BQ; in AUSTRALIA AND THE SOUTH PACIFIC by T.F.H. (Australia), Pty. Ltd., Box 149, Brookvale 2100 N.S.W., Australia; in NEW ZEALAND by Brooklands Aquarium Ltd. 5 McGiven Drive, New Plymouth, RD1 New Zealand; in Japan by T.F.H. Publications, Japan—Jiro Tsuda, 10-12-3 Ohjidai, Sakura, Chiba 285, Japan; in SOUTH AFRICA by Lopis (Pty) Ltd., P.O. Box 39127, Booysens, 2016, Johannesburg, South Africa. Published by T.F.H. Publications, Inc.
MANUFACTURED IN THE UNITED STATES OF AMERICA
BY T.F.H. PUBLICATIONS, INC.

ABYSSINIANS
Ruth Cooke-Zimmermann

What Is an Abyssinian Cat?

The history of the Abyssinian cat as we know it today is most controversial. Stories have our Abys coming from many parts of the world; it is even claimed that they are direct descendants of the big jungle cats. However, if we examine the ancient Egyptian works of art and artifacts, as well as the hieroglyphics, it is very clear that Abyssinians were the sacred cats of Egypt, so sacred that stories tell of their being buried with their masters as prized possessions.

The Abyssinian was first recognized in England in 1882. The first Abyssinian born in America was kittened in 1935 and was named Addis Ababa. The history of the breed is difficult to outline for the simple reason that no one bothered to write about it. During World War II, many Abys were shipped out of England to other countries to prevent destruction of the breed. It wasn't until after the war that their popularity grew, both as beautiful show cats and as devoted companions.

Abyssinian kittens are beautiful from birth. They are born with little pencil marks on their tiny faces; they have little white chins and soft chinchilla-like fur. For the first two weeks, all they do is eat and sleep, growing all the while. Promptly at three weeks of age, they pop out of the nesting box to explore the outside world and begin their

happy, inquisitive kitten life. They are such contented kittens from birth that I have actually heard many two-week-old litters purr while nursing. Once they are steady on their legs, Aby kittens are very active and playful, interested in all that goes on around them. This natural inquisitiveness is a part of the Aby standard.

Abyssinian kittens seem to mature earlier than other breeds. They play and begin to eat mild-flavored cat food usually as soon as they leave the nesting box. They are quite fearless and do love to be held and loved, purring loudly in response. For the most part, however, Abys have quiet voices when compared with other breeds. Some females in season don't even call, making it difficult to know when they should be mated.

While still very young, each kitten should be stroked and talked to softly; when they leave the nesting box, they should be fondled a bit each day to help them become used to people. They respond to love at a very young age and will be your friends forever. While you are holding each one, talk to it softly.

Opposite: The Abyssinian is considered by many to be a direct descendent of the sacred cat of Egypt.

Soon it will respond by purring and arching its little back in the typical Aby pose.

Now is the time to supply them with some safe toys. Your local pet shop or cat show booth will have a large collection of safe, fun toys from which to choose. In addition, Abys especially love Ping-Pong® balls and will bat them all over; all my cats and kittens prefer the yellow balls to the white. A low scratching post will give them hours of fun and teach them where they should exercise their claws. I buy packages of colorful boys' crew socks, stretch each sock out (after washing, of course), and then keep tying each one into a tight knot. These sock knots make virtually indestructible toys (even my dogs play with them) and can be put into the washer and dryer when they get dirty. My cats toss them all over the

Ch. Purssynian's Pink Floyd of Ming-Tai, fawn Abyssinian bred by Beth and Darrell Newkirk and owned by Ruth Cooke-Zimmermann. You may find that your Aby is a ping-pong lover, too.

Purssynian's Kanga Bloo, four-month-old blue Aby bred and owned by Beth and Darrell Newkirk.

house and have a great time. Before giving any furry toy mice to my Abys, I remove the eyes, whiskers, tails, ears, and anything else that can be pulled off and swallowed.

Some Abyssinians in the U.S.A. have changed in appearance very drastically over the past few years. Not all breeders have taken to the new style, but many have. If you go to a cat show you may watch a class of Abys, some of which look very much like the Siamese. Most are still the beauties we all love, with their pretty rounded heads, plush coats, and huge golden eyes. The new type has a very short slick coat and looks very extreme; some individual cats are having all kinds of health problems.

When you see a gorgeous ticked cat with vibrant coloring; a soft lustrous coat; brilliant gold almond-shaped eyes; pencil markings emphasizing the beauty of the sweet face; a soft bird-like voice; an extremely alert and intelligent expression, looking very much like a small puma—this is an Abyssinian, a joy to own and a rare beauty indeed!

TEMPERAMENT AND DISPOSITION

Abyssinians have a temperament and disposition like no other breed—they are cats that live to be loved. They don't care if you are reading, typing,

Left: Keep in mind that all Abys are individuals with unique personalities. ***Opposite:*** *Ch. Bromide Neptunium, bred and owned by Kate and Karl Faler.*

writing, sewing, knitting, eating, sleeping, or any of these "inconsequential" things; if they want to be loved and petted, they want it right then—no matter how busy you might be! They won't give up until you cease what you are doing and give them your full attention and love.

Abyssinians love to cuddle in your lap, sit on your shoulder, sleep right beside you or on your pillow and above your head. They are "people" cats and delightful companions. They will play with you with a favorite toy until you are exhausted, and they never seem to tire. They are so tuned in to people that they sense your every mood. If you feel sad or blue, they try to let you know that they are there to comfort you, and they will lick your cheek and cuddle close to you to let you know they care.

Aby kittens are very playful, but not in a destructive way. Adult Abys always keep their playful ways too, but they are quiet and well behaved. All Abys love to play fetch and can learn tricks very quickly. I have owned several other breeds of cat throughout the years, but I have found no other that has such a fantastic intelligence, temperament and disposition. For a delightful, affectionate, playful, intelligent, alert, constantly purring, exquisitely beautiful companion, an Abyssinian is what you want!

Abyssinian Standards

For many, many years we had only two colors of Abyssinians, Ruddy and Red; now we have the newcomers, Blue and Fawn. The two new colors have caused quite a bit of controversy among Aby lovers and breeders. Clubs for the advancement of each new color have been started all over the world, and both have been accepted in some associations already. Quite a few lovely Blue and Fawn Grand Champions and regional winners have been recorded. As in every other breed, certain people like only certain colors, and the new colors have had a hard time being accepted after all the years of only Ruddy and Red. Believe it or not, many breeders don't even care for the exquisitely beautiful Red Abys. Many think that the Ruddy is the only Aby to own. It is the same in the Siamese breed. With the multitude of colors now accepted for showing, most people still prefer the Seal Point cats. I guess old habits are hard to break.

Red and blue Abyssinian kittens owned by Sheila Dentico.

Ming-Tai's Eddie (breeder Ruth Cooke-Zimmermann, owner Dawn Grubb), ruddy male Aby, with his canine pal Chili. Dogs and cats that are properly introduced can become the best of friends, especially if they meet at a young age.

Some breeders are so violently put off by the new colors of Blue and Fawn that they are bombarding all Aby breeders with very lengthy letters trying to prove that these new color Abyssinians are not Abyssinians at all.

I feel that all Abys are gorgeous. Their color does not change their loving, sweet dispositions in any way, and if a person prefers to buy and love a Blue or Fawn Aby, he should be allowed to do so in peace. I feel "to each his own"!! Progress can't be stopped by closed-minded individuals. The cat fancy is also a democracy!

I am using The International Cat Association Standards for all four colors, since the Association accepts them all to be shown to multiple Grand. The Abyssinian Standards are as follows:

Despite the acceptance of blue and fawn Abyssinians, ruddy and red are still the most popular Aby colors.

HEAD.. 25 Points
    Profile 5
    Muzzle 5
    Skull 5
    Ears 5
    Eye Shape 5
COAT AND TEXTURE.. 10 Points
BODY.. 30 Points
    Torso 15
    Legs and Feet 10
    Tail 5
COLOR AND PATTERN... 35 Points
    Color... 15
    Ticking 15
    Eye Color... 5

General: The overall impression of the ideal Abyssinian is a medium to large cat, regal in appearance. Males proportionately larger than females, the female being finer boned and usually more active than the male. The Abyssinian shows firm muscular development and is lithe and panther-like in activity, showing a lively interest in all surroundings. The coat of the Abyssinian has an iridescent quality reflecting warmth of color, giving the impression of a colorful cat. Coat pattern is genetically a form of agouti ticking, with even dark-colored ticking contrasted with lighter bands, giving a translucent effect. The Abyssinian is of sound health and vigor, well-balanced physically and temperamentally gentle and amenable to handling.

Head: Modified wedge with rounded contours as viewed from the front. In profile without flat planes, showing gently curved transition between brow, nose and muzzle. A rise from the bridge of the nose to the forehead without evidence of a sharp break. The head should be of ample length in general balance with the rest of the cat, with width between the ears and gently curved from the forehead over the skull flowing into an arched neck.

Muzzle: The muzzle shall follow gentle contours in conformity with the head as viewed from the front and in profile. Chin shall be full and neither projecting nor receding, having a rounded appearance. Allowance made for jowls in adult males. The muzzle shall not be sharply pointed and there shall be no evidence of snipiness, foxy appearance or whisker pinch.

Ears: Large, alert, and moderately pointed, broad and cupped at base and arched forward, set as though listening. Hair on ears short and close lying, preferably tipped in conformity with the color requirements. A "thumb print" marking is desirable on the back of the ear.

Eyes: Almond shaped, large, brilliant and expressive. Skull aperture follows almond shape of eyes, being neither round nor oriental. Eyes accentuated by darkened lid skin, encircled by a light-colored area. Above each eye appears a short vertical darker pencil stroke amidst the lighter area. At the sides of each eye appears a curved darker pencil line as if a continuation of the upper lid.

Body: Medium length, lithe and graceful, showing well developed muscular strength without coarseness, and solid to the feel. The rib cage is rounded with no evidence of flat sides. The back is slightly arched, giving the appearance of a cat about to spring. The flank shall be reasonably level without tuck up. Conformation strikes a medium between the extremes of cobby and svelte lengthy type. Proportion and general balance to be desired more than mere size.

Legs: Proportionately slim; however, well muscled. The Abyssinian stands well off the ground and the length of leg should be in proportion with the length of body.

Feet: Oval and compact. When standing, giving the impression of being on tip toe.

Tail: Thick at base, fairly long and tapering.

Coat and Texture: Coat dense and resilient to the touch, with a lustrous sheen, fine in texture. Medium length, long enough to accommodate four or six alternating light and dark-colored bands. The coat lies fairly close to the body; however, the undercoat should be adequate enough to avoid any evidence of slickness. Wooliness undesirable. Coat is longest at the spine, gradually shortening over the saddle, flank, legs and head.

Disqualify: White locket or white anywhere on the body other than around nostril, chin and upper throat areas. Unbroken necklace. Deformed feet. Reversed ticking (outermost tip of hair light instead of dark), wrong color or patching in pads,

wrong color coat for color requirements.

Penalize: COLOR FAULTS— Cold, grey or sandy tone to coat color. Black or grey hair next to skin with absence of proper undercoat. Broken necklaces, leg bars, mottling or speckling in unticked areas (underside of body, chest and inside legs), tabby stripes or bars. Slick coat or excessive plushiness a fault. TICKING AND PATTERN FAULTS— Unevenness of ticking over body, lack of desired markings on head and tail.

Condition: There is no point score for condition as such. Flabbiness of body, lack of coat lustre, eye color, evidence of illness, emaciation and lack of muscle tone are faults and points shall be deducted under the various headings constituting the point score.

Color Division: Recognized in Tabby Color Division, Ruddy, Sorrel (Red), Blue, and Fawn.

Note: It is noted in the standards of most associations that since Abyssinians don't reach their full potential until the age of 18 months, judges give consideration to this fact when judging color, ticking, and style.

RUDDY
Color: Orange-brown (burnt sienna), ticked with two or three bands of either black or dark brown, the extreme outer tip to be the darkest with orange-

An unusual "rainbow" litter—red, blue, ruddy, and fawn—bred by Cornelia Tichenor. Parents of this colorful brood are Ch. Dearabi Hill Street (sire) and Dearabi Chobkis (dam).

brown to the skin. Outer parts of the body covered by shorter hair shall not have less than one band of ticking. Darker shadings along spine allowed if fully ticked. The undersides of the body, chest, and the insides of the legs to be an even orange-brown without ticking, barring, necklaces or belly marks. Lighter shades of orange-brown in deeper shades. White or off-white to be confined only to the upper throat, lips and nostril area. Tail to be tipped with black, without rings or grey tones.

Paw pads: Black or dark brown with black between toes and extending slightly beyond paws.

Eye color: Gold, green or hazel, the more richness and depth of color the better.

Nose Leather: Brick tile red.

RED (SORREL) ABYSSINIAN

Color: A dilution of the ruddy, being a warm sorrel red ticked with chocolate brown. Tail tipped with chocolate brown. Preference given to deeper shades of sorrel and good even ticking.

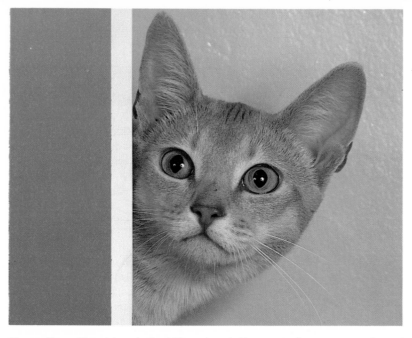

Above: Fawn Abyssinian playing hide-and-seek. Fawns are the newest members of the Aby family, although several other colors are being developed in the U.S. and Great Britain. Owner, Diane Jackson. *Below:* The coat color of the blue Abyssinian is a warm, soft blue ticked with deeper blue, with the chest and inside of legs a warm cream color. Owner, Sheila Dentico.

Paw pads: Pink with chocolate brown between toes, extending slightly beyond paws.

Eye color: Gold, green or hazel, the more richness and depth of color the better.

Nose leather: Rosy pink.

BLUE ABYSSINIAN

Color: A warm soft blue ticked with deeper blue. Undersides of the body, chest and inside of legs to be a warm cream color. Tail tipped with a deep shade of blue. Preference to be given to good even ticking.

Paw pads: Blue with a deep shade of blue between the toes extending slightly beyond the paws.

Eye color: Gold, copper, green or hazel, the more richness and depth of color the better.

Nose leather: Dark pink.

FAWN ABYSSINIAN

Color: A warm pinkish buff with powdered effect ticked with deeper shade of pinkish buff. Base hair, undersides of body, chest and inside of legs to be pale oatmeal. Spine shading to be a darker shade of body color. Tail tipped with a deep shade of pinkish buff. Preference given to good even ticking.

Paw pads: Pink-mauve with a deep pinkish buff between toes extending slightly beyond paws.

Eye color: Gold, copper, green or hazel, the more richness and depth of color the better.

Nose leather: Pink-mauve.

Gr. Ch. Izod's First Star, owned by Marti Higgins. All Abyssinians give the overall impression of nobility and grace, and they make a lasting impression on everyone they meet.

The Somali

When you see a cat with the sweet beautiful face of the Abyssinian, complete with pencil markings but with longer, soft hair and a big bushy tail, this is the longhaired Aby—the Somali.

For many years Aby breeders had an occasional kitten with strange long hair in a litter; these kittens were given away as pets. Finally their beauty was recognized, and the pioneers of the breed started breeding them true and named them Somali. They are beautiful animals with the same sweet disposition and temperament of the Aby, but with longer hair. In one association Somalis are judged in the same class as the Abyssinian. The following is the standard for the Somali.

SOMALI STANDARD

General: The overall impression of the ideal Somali is that of a well proportioned, medium to large cat, firm muscular development, lithe, showing an alert, lively interest in all surroundings, with an even disposition, and easy to handle.

Skull: A modified, slightly rounded wedge without flat planes; the brow, cheek, and profile lines all showing a gentle contour; a slight rise from the bridge of the nose to the forehead, which should be of good size, with width between the ears flowing into the arched neck without a break.

Muzzle: The muzzle shall follow gentle contours in conformity with the skull as viewed from the front profile. Chin shall be full, neither undershot nor overshot, having a rounded appearance. The muzzle shall not be sharply pointed and there shall be no evidence of snipiness, foxiness or whisker pinch. Allowance is to be made for jowls in adult males.

Ears: Large, alert, moderately pointed; broad and cupped at the base. Ear set on a line toward the rear of the skull. The inner ear shall have horizontal tufts that reach nearly to the other side of the ear; tufts desirable.

Eye shape: Almond shaped, large, brilliant and expressive. Skull aperture neither round nor oriental. Eyes accented by dark lidskin, encircled by light-colored area. Above each eye a short dark vertical pencil stroke with a dark pencil line continuing from the upper lid toward the ear.

Eye color: Gold or green, the more richness and depth of color the better.

Body: Torso medium long, lithe and graceful, showing well-developed muscular strength. Rib cage rounded, back is

Opposite: A striking ruddy Somali, a longhaired Abyssinian.

slightly arched, giving appearance of a cat about to spring; flank level with no tuck-up. Conformation strikes a medium between the extremes of cobby and svelte lengthy types.

Legs and feet: Legs in proportion to torso; feet oval and compact. When standing, the Somali gives the impression of being nimble and quick. Toes—five in front and four behind.

Tail: Having a full brush, thick at the base and slightly tapering. Length in balance with torso.

Coat color: RUDDY—Overall impression is of an orange-brown or ruddy color ticked with black. Color has radiant or glowing quality. Darker shading along the spine allowed. Underside of body and inside of legs and chest to be an even ruddy tone harmonizing with top coat, without ticking, barring, necklaces, or belly marks. Nose leather tile red; paw pads black

The Somali's conformation strikes a balance between the extremes of cobby and svelte body types.

The Somali now comes in the same four colors as the Abyssinian. Owner, Margery S. Hoff.

or dark brown, with black between toes and extending upward on rear of legs. Toe tufts on front and rear feet black or dark brown. White or off-white on upper throat, lips and nostrils only. Tail continuing the dark spine line, ending at black at the tip. Complete absence of rings on tail. Preference given to unmarked Ruddy color. Ears tipped with black or dark brown.

RED—Warm glowing red, ticked with chocolate brown. Deeper shades of red preferred. Ears and tail tipped with chocolate brown. Paw pads pink, with chocolate brown toes,

extending slightly beyond paws. Nose leather rosy pink.

BLUE—Warm soft blue ticked with deeper blue. Undersides of the body, chest, and insides of legs to be a warm cream color. Tail tipped with a deep shade of blue. Preference to be given to good even ticking. Paw pads blue with a deep shade of blue between the toes extending slightly beyond the paws. Eye color gold, copper, green, or hazel, the more richness and depth of color the better. Nose leather dark pink.

FAWN—Warm pinkish buff with powdered effect ticked with

Gr. Ch. Winery's Tavel of Duracell, bred by Carol Harrison and owned by Gale Taylor. It is important to note that the Somali is slow to show mature ticking; therefore, allowances should be made for the coloring of kittens and young adults.

deeper shade of pinkish buff. Base hair, undersides of body, chest, and insides of legs to be pale oatmeal. Spine shading to be a darker shade of body color. Tail tipped with a deep shade of pinkish buff. Preference given to good even ticking. Paw pads pink-mauve with a deep pinkish buff between toes extending slightly beyond paws. Eye color gold, copper, green, or hazel, the more richness and depth of color the better. Nose leather pink-mauve.

Ticking: Beginning at skin with ruddy tone alternating with black for ruddies. Beginning at skin, with red tones alternating with chocolate brown for reds.

Please note that the Somali is extremely slow in showing mature ticking, so allowance should be made for kittens and very young adult cats.

Texture: Very soft to the touch, extremely fine and double coated. The more dense the coat the better.

Length: A medium length coat except over shoulders, where a slightly shorter length is permitted. Preference is to be given to a cat with ruff and breeches, giving a full appearance to the cat.

Condition: The cat to give the appearance of activity, sound health and general vigor.

Penalize: COLOR FAULTS—Cold grey or sandy tone to coat color; mottling or speckling on unticked areas. PATTERN FAULTS—Necklaces, leg barring, tabby stripes or bars on body; lack of desired markings on head and tail. Black roots on body.

Withhold winners: Withhold winners ribbons for white lockets or groin spot or white anywhere on body other than nostrils, chin and upper throat; any skeletal abnormalities; wrong color in paw pads or nose leather; unbroken necklaces; incorrect number of toes; kinks in tail.

A red Somali, Duracell Peaches, bred and owned by Gale Taylor. The overall impression of the Somali is a cat of activity, sound health, and vigor.

Buying an Abyssinian

You can choose among several places to buy an Abyssinian. You may call local vets for names of people who breed Abys. It's also possible to find a beautiful healthy Aby in a pet shop. If not, the owner may know of a breeder in your area.

The various cat associations will give you a list of breeders in your area if you request it. Classified ads for felines appear in all cat publications. If you know of anyone who is fortunate enough to own an Aby, ask where he found his cat and if he would recommend the same place to you. If there are any cat shows in your area, go to see if any breeders have any kittens with them that are for sale. Some breeders do sell their best kittens at shows, but even if they don't have kittens available, they may know where you can find one. If the breeders you speak to are showing cats that you find very attractive and have good dispositions, ask to be put on a waiting list. Most good breeders do have waiting lists, so the sooner your name is on one, the sooner you will be the proud owner of a beautiful Aby kitten.

When you buy from a breeder, you can see how the kitten was raised, talk to the breeder, and see the kitten's parents, and possibly other kittens or cats from these same lines. If the house is clean, the kittens healthy, the sire and dam friendly and outgoing, you stand a good chance of getting a kitten with a good disposition, since disposition and temperament, as well as beauty, are inherited. If the kittens are friendly, outgoing, inquisitive, and purring, they have been properly "peoplized" and should make you happy.

Don't buy a kitten too young, no matter how adorable it is. This is most important. Some disreputable breeders over-breed their females as often as possible, and they sell the kittens at five or six weeks of age just to escape the expense of giving them their most important shots and love. It is best for both mother and kitten if they nurse a full eight weeks. If the kittens don't, they might chew on everything in sight, even you. Their sucking instincts must be satisfied if they are to become happy, healthy adults.

Abyssinian kittens should be strong and healthy, inquisitive and outgoing, have soft lustrous coats, be free of fleas and fungus, and have clear, bright eyes that are free of any discharge. Don't choose a kitten that runs away from you and doesn't want to be touched,

Opposite: *The most important step toward purchasing a beautiful, healthy Aby is locating a reputable source.*

because it may have a problem. It might just be temporarily shy, but you have to be the judge in observing it. You certainly want the happiest, healthiest kitten you can find.

A kitten should not go to a new home until it is at least 11 or 12 weeks of age. It should have had its all-important shots, should be eating a variety of foods, and should be litter trained. Whether you plan to buy your kitten with a form to register it or not, the breeder should give you a copy of the kitten's pedigree. You should also receive the name and date of shots given and by whom, so you will know when to schedule the kitten's yearly booster. You should also receive a list of the foods the kitten has been eating and a feeding schedule. Try to stick to these foods and this schedule to help your kitten settle in well and to prevent tummy upsets.

Most reputable breeders want you to take your kitten to a good vet for a check-up 12 to 48 hours

Newly arrived and in quarantine, fourteen-week-old ruddy Aby sisters Lohrengel Shalimar of Ming-Tai and Lohrengel Salome of Ming-Tai, bred by Maja Lohrengel and owned by Ruth Cooke-Zimmermann. Never purchase a kitten younger than 11 or 12 weeks of age.

Ming-Tai's Eddie with pal Chili. Breeder, Ruth Cooke-Zimmermann; owner, Dawn Grubb.

after purchase. Take a stool sample for the vet to check. If worms are found, the proper medication will be available to you. Never buy advertised medicine and try to worm your kitten or cat yourself. You have to know what kind of worm is present and treat it according to your vet's instructions. Treating your kitten or cat with the wrong medication could prove fatal. Having your kitten checked right away will help you get established with your vet before you have an emergency—and I hope you will never have one. Abys are healthy cats, but it is

important to locate and become familiar with a good vet as soon as possible. Make sure your vet likes cats. You will need his services for your Aby's regular booster shots and for spaying or neutering your pet. If you don't already have a vet, ask your cat-owning friends for their recommendations. Pet Abys are usually sold with a spay or neuter agreement that makes them less expensive than a breeder or show cat.

If a breeder tries to sell you a very young kitten as "top show quality" at a greatly inflated price, beware. Abyssinians don't

A mother Aby and two of her beautiful offspring. Owner, JoAnn M. Laub. It is a good idea to see your prospective pet's mother and father, if at all possible. This way, you can get an idea of how your kitten will look when it is grown.

reach their full potential until they are 18 months of age. Until that time they will be constantly changing. The "beauty" may become a disappointment as far as looks and color are concerned, but that loving disposition will never change unless the cat is mistreated. The "ugly duckling" might blossom into a most beautiful cat, a vision of beauty that might well become a Grand Champion if you show it. This has happened to all breeders. I kept a female from one of my litters, even though she was very pale in color when she was little. She had a super pedigree, so I watched her to see what would happen. As the weeks progressed it didn't look as if she would change, but all of a sudden she developed a vibrant coloring, and she grew more beautiful every day. I knew by her background that this should happen, but it could just as well have gone the other way.

Abys are very tricky this way. One day you look at them, and a few days later they look completely different, so it is impossible to say that a very young kitten will be "top" show quality. If you are considering buying an Aby to show, study the pedigree, observe the sire and dam and any other cats from this same breeding that the breeder might still have, and then just hope for the best.

MALE OR FEMALE?

Most people have the mistaken idea that female cats are more affectionate and playful than males. In the Abyssinian breed, this is not true. The males are every bit as lovable, playful, and cuddly as the females are. Your male should be neutered as soon as his testicles are fully descended if you don't plan to breed him. Your vet will tell you when he is ready, but don't wait until the animal starts to spray all over your house, or you will be sorry. Don't let him have "just one litter" as a lot of people think is "best," because once he has started his sex life, he may spray even after he is neutered. There is nothing as unpleasant smelling as a spraying whole male Abyssinian loose in your home. He can ruin your drapes, furniture, rugs, and anything he chooses to spray on.

If you plan to use your male as a stud, get him used to being caged before he starts to spray or you won't be able to stand the smell. The spray is overpowering, to say the least, and it is also very dangerous. Males can spray a long distance, and if the spray hits an electrical socket, a heater, or any electrical appliance that is plugged in, you could have a disastrous fire. The spray works just like a wick works with dynamite. Many breeders have lost their entire homes, cats and all, before this was recognized as the cause. Females may spray when in season, and, although it is not so odoriferous, it is just as deadly.

If you don't plan to breed and want a contented male, do have him neutered as soon as your vet says it is time. It is cruel to keep an unaltered Aby male as a pet, because when he matures, he will have one thing on his mind, and your previously happy and contented pet can become very frustrated and unhappy. An altered pet, male or female, is so much happier and nicer to have around. Neutering a male is a much simpler procedure than spaying a female, so I usually recommend a male as a pet to be neutered. Usually you drop him off at the vet's office in the morning (he must have an empty stomach), and pick him up in late afternoon of the same day. He just has to be watched to prevent falling if the anesthesia

A trio of six-week-old blue female Aby kittens, bred and owned by Beth and Darrell Newkirk.

A trio of Somali kittens. A healthy kitten is one that is active, alert, and aware of its surroundings.

hasn't completely worn off. By the next day, he's right back to normal.

If you buy a female and don't plan to breed her, it is only fair to her to have her spayed. If she is allowed to be constantly in season, she will probably stop eating and lose weight, making her more apt to pick up any airborne illness in her weakened state. Being continually in season can really wear your female Aby down. She can develop cystic ovaries which will call for an operation anyway. It is

better not to wait until she is run down and ill, but have her spayed as soon as your vet says she is ready.

A neutered Aby is a contented, happy Aby, male or female, and will be a more lovable pet than ever, if that's possible.

Neutered or, as they are called, altered Abys may be shown in the Alter Class at cat shows, as long as they have not been de-clawed, and can become Premiers or Grand Premiers. If your neutered Aby is a real beauty and meets the Aby

Blue female kittens bred and owned by Cornelia Tichenor. If you feel you don't have enough time to spend with your new Aby, why not get two? A pair of Abyssinians will keep each other busy and out of mischief.

standard, you might enjoy showing it and having a top winner!

TRY A PAIR OF ABYS

You have heard the jingle about "double the pleasure—double the fun." This is true of two Abys rather than one!

Many people worry about leaving their new Aby kitten alone while they are at work all day, especially if they work long hours and have a long commute. Two Aby kittens, especially from the same litter, may be your answer. They have been together since birth and, therefore, they don't feel as strange in a new home. They are used to playing, eating, and sleeping together, and do adapt much quicker to a new situation because they are together. Two kittens eat better, use their new litter box sooner, and are happy just to be together. Believe me—watching them play is better than TV. You will be rewarded with twice as much love, companionship and joy from a pair of Abys.

THE NEW HOME

Try to have everything you will need for your new Aby kitten ready before you pick it up. It is best to keep the kitten in a small bedroom or a warm bathroom with its litter, food, water, bed, and toys for a few days until it becomes accustomed to the new surroundings, noises, and smells. Play with the kitten often to make it feel at home so it will get used to you. Many Aby kittens will enter a new home and act as if they had always lived there. So much the better for you.

Be sure you have a cat carrier in which to bring home your new Aby, because you should never transport your kitten or cat without one. Some people think it is cute to have a kitten or cat loose in the car, but a sudden

Your cat should be groomed on a regular basis to keep it looking its best. A variety of shampoos are available at your local pet shop. Photo courtesy of Four Paws.

loud noise such as that of a truck or a motorcycle might frighten it, and if it starts flying around the car in fright, it could cause a disastrous accident. Your Aby may cry or try hard to get out of the carrier the first few times, but it will soon become used to it if you don't give in and take it out. Put a soft towel in the bottom of the carrier along with a toy, and talk to the kitten reassuringly. Many Aby owners leave the carrier open at home and the Aby sleeps or plays in it. This way the cat is accustomed to it when it's time to travel. It is the only safe way for an Aby or any cat to leave its home.

Before you bring your new Aby kitten home, pick out a nice warm sunny spot for its bed, although it will probably rather sleep with you. If you allow this, make sure it learns how to get up and down from the bed—you wouldn't want it to fall and get hurt. Be sure the room is warm and free from drafts, since shorthaired cats like warmth. In addition, teach it to go up and down stairs if it is not used to them.

A scratching post is a must if you want to protect your furniture and drapes when the kitten has the run of the house. Scratching posts come in a great variety of styles, so you can get more than one at a reasonable price. They are available at pet shops and shows, and range

Have a sleeping spot and a bed ready and waiting before bringing your new Aby home. Cat beds are available at your local pet shop. These three-month-old blue Abyssinian kittens bred and owned by Maja Lohrengel.

Scratching posts offer hours of healthy exercise and enjoyment for cats and kittens while preventing them from damaging the furniture. Photo courtesy of Cosmic Pet Products.

from very small to ceiling high, with many styles in between. I don't advise ceiling high posts until your Aby is older; then they are great fun and exercise.

Another very useful and enjoyable thing to have for your Aby is a carpeted window perch. It can be moved from window to window to follow the sun, or may be permanently attached to a window. All Abys love to sprawl out on the perch in the warm sun.

By now you will have a litter box and litter. I use dishpans as litter boxes since they are deep enough to prevent a "super-digger" from spreading the litter all over the area. They are also very easy to keep clean. There are many types of litter on the market, but I use shredded paper, as do most vets. New

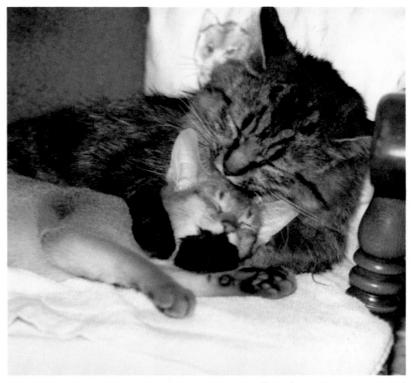

Ming-Tai's Eddie with his pal Julio the cat. Bred by Ruth Cooke-Zimmermann and owned by Dawn Grubb.

baby kittens just out of the nesting box love to stuff their little mouths with clay litter, and it frightens me to think what this could do to their tummies and intestines. It could cause a serious blockage and a very sick Aby. I have had to clean out too many little mouths full of litter, so I switched to paper with very good results. In addition, paper doesn't get tracked all over the house or ground into the floors when stepped on, and, best of all, it isn't dusty.

You should have a good supply of the foods from the list that the breeder gave you, food and water dishes, and plenty of safe toys. Abys, as well as all cats, love cat beds, and they are good for keeping your new kitten out of drafts, but make very sure the kind you get can't be chewed and cause a problem for your kitten's insides.

If you are bringing your new Aby into a home with other cats, introduce them gradually, as you would a new baby. The older cat or cats may hiss and growl at the new addition, but be sure to show the older ones that you still love them and that they are not being replaced in your affections. Most new kittens are accepted, with your help—some immediately, some in a few days. Unfortunately, some older, "spoiled" cats never really accept a newcomer, but the vast majority do delight in having a new young friend to frolic with.

If you bring your new acquisition into a home with other cats, you are best advised to "quarantine" the new Aby for a week or two. Every household has what are called "well germs," and every one has a different type. This doesn't mean that either your new Aby or your other cats are ill, but for some reason, these "well germs" can cause an upper respiratory illness, and you certainly don't want sick cats. Additionally, by quarantining your new Aby, if any of the other cats are harboring a disease of some sort, the new Aby shouldn't get it.

I had a very bad experience years ago when I bought a very beautiful show Siamese kitten,

and being then a novice, I put the kitten with all my other Siamese, and all the females were pregnant. The new kitten was sneezing, so I took her immediately to my vet, and since she was eating and playing well, he said she had an allergy. Unfortunately, she actually had rhinotracheitis, a serious upper respiratory illness now prevented

Somali kitten. If you are adding a kitten to a household with other pets, it is best to quarantine the youngster for a week or two.

by vaccine, and all of my Siamese got it. All of my pregnant females lost their kittens, and every cat, despite my vet's best care, developed pneumonia. Thankfully, they were all strong enough to recover with no ill effects. The kitten immediately went back to the breeder, but the damage was done, and we had many weeks of grief and very sick cats. Fortunately, the new quadruple shots now prevent this disease as well as others, but at that time they were not yet available. So do quarantine, even if you think it isn't necessary.

Since Aby kittens are usually very outgoing and friendly, even to the point of being fearless, they adapt very quickly to a new home. If yours doesn't eat or use the litter pan for a couple of days, don't worry, because soon nature will take its course. Abys are very rarely finicky eaters, so if you give them the foods they are used to, they will soon eat you out of house and home. If you start right out by feeding them from the table all kinds of things they shouldn't have, then you will have a problem. Stick to the regular diet. This is very important to the health of your new Aby.

Don't let your family and friends constantly handle your kitten until it has become accustomed to its new surroundings. In addition, keep people who have cats at home that might be ill away from your new pet, since germs can be carried on clothing, hands, shoes, and even hair.

When your new kitten is between four or five months of age you may see a spot of blood on a toy or find a tooth on the floor. Don't panic! This is the time that kittens lose their baby teeth. Many kittens may sneeze or have watery eyes while teething, but others never show any trace of being uncomfortable. Offer a spoon handle to chew on, or better yet, buy the smallest size puppy Nylabone® and keep it handy. It seems to help and it protects your fingers. A vet I used to have years ago, who has now retired, told me that a human could not stand the pain that a kitten or puppy goes through while teething. So, if your new Aby kitten is off its feed for a few days, be patient and offer it its favorite soft food. The kitten may run a slight fever, but don't try to help it by giving it either aspirin or Tylenol®, as both are poisonous to cats. Give your vet a call if the kitten acts too uncomfortable.

Opposite: Purrsynian's Quintessence, a seven-week-old blue Aby, bred and owned by Beth and Darrell Newkirk.

Feeding Your Abyssinian

When you bring your new Abyssinian home, you should have a list of its favorite foods and how much and when to feed it. Many new owners are so thrilled with their beautiful new kitten that they ignore the breeder's instructions and immediately start feeding the little pet the wrong things. Stick to the foods and schedule the kitten or cat is used to; this will save a lot of grief.

I have been to several seminars on feline nutrition, and at every one have learned that *cat* food is for cats, not people food. Read the labels on the food and get the food highest in protein, not a cheap food that is loaded with cereal. A steady diet of cheap food will give you a fat, unhealthy Aby with a dull coat and health and reproduction problems.

All of my cats used to have a can of the best cat food every morning, and the best dry food in the evening. Now I find that they are all leaving the canned food, so I have put them all on a steady diet of this super dry food, and they are all blossoming. This food comes in two types, one for kittens and pregnant Abys, and another for adult cats. My Abys love it. Just make sure they always have plenty of fresh water with any dry food. Occasionally I offer them the canned food they used to love, but now they won't even touch it. This is a complete cat food, and nothing extra is necessary; it is also very good for their teeth. It was formulated by vets and is well-balanced and either low in ash or ash-free, depending on which brand is available in your area. I sprinkle brewer's yeast powder on the dry food and mix it in a bit to provide the B vitamins that are so good for cats.

If you never see your cat or kitten drink water and the level in the water dish stays the same, sprinkle a bit of salt on the food to make him thirsty. Water is very necessary to the good health of your Aby. Some Aby owners give their cats and kittens vinegar and other such things to try to make them thirsty, but this could cause problems. Better to discuss this with your vet and follow his directions if you have a "water-hater."

I have never fed any of my Abys tuna or fish mixture foods. These have too much ash and cause kidney problems if the Aby doesn't drink enough water. There is a wide variety of meat, chicken, egg, and cheese mixtures available. Read the labels to be sure your Aby is

Opposite: Kitten owned by Dean Mastrangelo. For the first few weeks of adjustment, try to feed your new pet the food he is used to.

getting all the nourishment it needs. You may save a few pennies on a cheap food, but you will be taking a chance on the health of your cat.

I don't give any of my Abys any liver foods until they are at least six months old, as liver can cause loose bowels in a young cat. Remember, good cat food contains the proper balanced nutrition your pet needs to be healthy and playful and live a long life.

At the nutritional seminars I have attended I learned that many cat owners try to save money by feeding their cats dog food. Dog food is low in the proteins our Abys need. Dogs

Treats can be provided on an occasional basis to help provide a little variety in the diet. Some treats act as a cleaning agent to help reduce tartar on the cat's teeth. Photo courtesy of Heinz.

A nutritious diet is imperative to the good health and longevity of your Abyssinian. This lovely Aby is owned by Linda B. Jones.

can't eat cat food because the protein content is too much for their kidneys and could cause them many problems. The formula for feeding is very easy to remember: people food for people, cat food for cats, and dog food for dogs. To each his own.

Many Aby owners feed their pets a steady diet of raw meat, but although the cats may love it, nutritionists and vets really frown on this because it is not the balanced diet our pets need. Despite whatever supplements you add, you don't have the proper balance for the needs of your cat.

I have found that if an Aby must have a pill of any kind, burying the pill in a very small meatball of raw lean ground beef or liverwurst works very well. The

Three-month-old red sisters, Ming-Tai's Amber Flame and Ming-Tai's Tawny Flame, bred and owned by Ruth Cooke-Zimmermann. If you have two or more Abys, be sure to provide enough food for each.

cat usually gobbles it right up, pill and all, and you don't have to struggle to get it down his throat. That small amount of raw meat is a treat, not a steady diet, and a very convenient way to dose an Aby when necessary. Soft cheese is also good to bury a pill in, as is a small bit of their favorite canned food.

Milk used to be "the thing" to give cats, but no more. Now, for some reason, the vast majority of cats get upset stomachs or loose bowels from milk or milk products. I only give milk to my Aby queens just before and just after delivering kittens. Then I use straight evaporated milk. This seems to help their own milk supply to come in, and it gives them back some of the energy lost in the delivery of the litter. If it upsets them, I stop it immediately.

Grooming Your Abyssinian

Due to their soft gleaming coats, Abys are very easy to groom. A quick brushing once a week with a soft natural bristle brush, to remove any loose hairs, and a quick clip of their claws with scissor-type clippers, to prevent accidents while at play, is just about all the grooming they need.

If you show your Abyssinian or if your Aby has gotten dirty somehow, you will want to bathe it. Abys love water-play, so they are usually very good at bath time.

First, assemble the things you will need for the bath: nail clippers to trim the nails first so you won't get scratched; large, soft towels; a good feline protein shampoo (diluted in a paper or plastic cup with water, making it easier to rinse out); a plastic container for rinsing the coat; a big apron for yourself; cotton-tipped cleaners for the Aby's outer ears; and a soft washcloth for washing its face.

Next, make very sure that the room is warm enough before starting the bath. I use my bathroom, with the door closed to keep the warmth (and the Aby) in. Fill the sink half full with lukewarm water. Test the temperature with your elbow to make sure it is not too hot. A sprayer attached to your sink will make your chore much easier.

Good grooming habits should start at an early age. Your pet shop can help you select the proper grooming aids for your cat. Photo courtesy of The Kong Company.

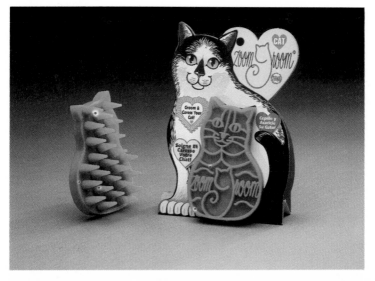

Grasp the cat's front legs with your left hand, with your index finger between them, and hold firmly; stand the hind legs in the sink, all the while talking softly to your Aby. Wash the face and ears with the face cloth, making very sure to avoid getting soap in the eyes or water in the ears (I use plain water on the face area). Wet the coat thoroughly, and apply a line of the diluted shampoo from the back of the head down the back to the tail. Continue talking softly and praising your Aby while working quickly and gently to lather the coat, including the hind end and tail as well as the feet, legs, tummy, and chest. Unless the cat is really dirty, one lathering is enough. Indoor cats very rarely get soiled. Gently squeeze off as much lather as possible while draining the wash water. Rinse the coat thoroughly. Rinsing out all the shampoo is very important, as the residue leaves a dull film on the coat and irritates the skin. When all the shampoo is out, the coat will gleam. I find that my Abys don't really like to be rinsed off, so instead of refilling the sink, I use the plastic container and continually pour clean water through the coat until all the shampoo is gone and the cat is squeaky clean. When you are sure all the shampoo is gone, try to squeeze as much water out of the coat as possible with your

hands. Wrap your clean Aby in a big towel and dry it as best you can, all the while talking to it and praising it. Using a hair dryer set on a low temperature is great if your Aby will tolerate it. Mine are afraid of the noise and the blowing air, so I dry them well with the towel. It is impossible to get the cat completely dry, but do the best you can. Keep the cat in the warm bathroom and he will finish the drying by licking himself. When completely dry, a quick brushing, along with a lot of praise, will make a happy, clean, gleaming Abyssinian very proud of itself!

It is always helpful, when bathing your Aby the first few times, to have an "assistant" standing by—someone your Aby likes and trusts. Unless you show your cat often, you shouldn't have to bathe it frequently, if at all.

If you find that your cats have picked up fleas somewhere, don't panic. Ask your vet for a good flea powder, sprinkle a line of it down the middle of the animal's back, and fluff it through the coat with your hands. Don't get it in the cat's face or eyes. In a few hours you should be able to brush the powder out, but follow your vet's instructions. The fleas "bite the dust" very quickly with this powder treatment. If necessary, you can repeat the treatment once a week until all the Abys

A trio of four-week-old ruddy kittens bred and owned by Marti Higgins. If you don't mind sharing your bed with your Aby, be sure to teach him how to get up and down safely.

are free of fleas, but don't use too much powder each time, as it is very powerful. Don't ever put flea powder on a sick or pregnant Aby; follow your vet's instructions if you have very young kittens with fleas. The fleas suck a lot of blood, and if there are enough of them they can cause severe anemia or even death in a very young kitten. Finally, be sure to sprinkle a bit of flea powder in the Aby's bed to destroy any possible inhabitant fleas.

As you can see, grooming an Abyssinian can't compare to grooming a longhaired cat. If your cat sheds a bit, in warm weather or when the heat is turned on for the winter months, and licks itself a lot, give it one of the several tube type hairball remedies, available at pet shops, once in a while to prevent hairballs from forming in the stomach. All cats preen themselves, but if you keep the loose hair brushed every week, you should have no problems with hairballs.

Health and Safety

Over the past few years, new immunizations have become available for our cats. They can now be protected from many of the dreaded diseases for which no protection was available in the past. Just a few years ago, just one panleukopenia shot was given to kittens at nine weeks of age, but now triple and quadruple shots are available to protect them from such diseases as rhinotracheitis, calicivirus, panleukopenia, and chlamydia. These shots are given at 6 or 9 weeks of age and 12 weeks later, with a booster shot every year thereafter. In many areas, and especially if you plan to take your Aby out of the country, a rabies shot is necessary. Some states now insist on rabies shots by law.

Somali kitten poking its nose where it doesn't belong. Always remember that Somalis and Abyssinians are very intelligent and, therefore, very curious cats.

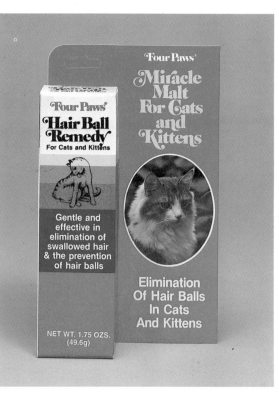

Products are available for aiding in the elimination of hairballs in cats and kittens. Photo courtesy of Four Paws.

A few years ago, there was only one test for feline leukemia virus. Now there are more available, even one that can be done in the vet's office. All cats should be periodically tested for this frightening disease, since some cats show no symptoms at all but are constantly shedding the virus much like "Typhoid Mary." Follow your vet's recommendation if you have a cat that tests positive. Fortunately for healthy, leukemia-free Abys, there are now vaccines to prevent this horrible disease. Ask your vet for information about this protection.

Abys and plants are mortal enemies—there are too many toxic plants to make keeping one worth the risk of your pet's life!

ABYS AND POISONOUS PLANTS AND PRODUCTS

Plants are the "in" way to decorate now, both indoors and out. Most of us love plants and plant stores are doing a booming business. Sad to say, many of these plants and flowers are poisonous to all cats. Leaves, stems, bulbs, berries, and blossoms can all kill if even a small bit is eaten by an Aby. You can't trust a cat or kitten not to touch a plant, because he will, and if it is a poisonous plant you could lose your beloved pet. A tiny bite is all it takes to cause you heartache and grief.

Philodendron of any kind is one of the most common house plants because it is so indestructible and beautiful, but it is also one of the most deadly. All parts of the plant contain crystals of calcium oxolate, which quickly kills a cat.

Caladium, dieffenbachia (or dumb cane, as it is often called), narcissus, jonquil, lily of the valley, azalea, four o'clock, wisteria, larkspur, iris, mountain laurel, and all of the dried decorative flowers and reeds used so much in silk flower displays are poisonous. Our popular holiday plants—holly, poinsettia, and all parts of mistletoe—are killers when eaten by our Abys. The list is very long, and our Abys cannot tell a safe plant from a killer.

I love plants, but I most definitely love my Abys more! I have only beautiful big silk plants all over my house—ferns, hanging baskets of silk philodendron and ivy and a large silk palm tree. They look just like real plants, but I know they are safe! You have to make the

Once again, plants and Abys don't mix! The only safe plants are silk or plastic plants.

decision of whether you want a houseful of dangerous plants or an Aby. If they meet, the plants will be the survivors!

Any kind of cleaner or spray cleaner that contains phenol is deadly to our Aby's entire nervous system, and many of the most popular brands have this product. Read the labels. Clorox® is great, but poisonous, and must be very well rinsed when used.

Keep all of your people medicines away from your Aby.

A good rule to follow is if the product says to keep away from children, keep it well away from your Aby too.

If your Aby should get hold of any poisonous substance at all, call your vet as fast as you can to save its life. Even if you aren't quite sure it was poison, call him anyway to be on the safe side.

KEEPING YOUR ABYSSINIAN SAFE

People asking to buy one of my beloved Abys know from the

Ruddy kitten owned by Dean Mastrangelo. Abys love to investigate; therefore, all toxic substances must always be out of reach of your Aby.

Purssynian Kookaburra, ruddy male owned by Beth and Darrell Newkirk. Abyssinians need to drink water—but not out of a faucet! If your pet seems reluctant to drink out of his bowl, try moving it to another spot.

very beginning of the conversation that if they plan to let it out of doors, they won't be able to buy a cat or kitten from me!! I have been told that they have a lot of land, they will keep the Aby on a leash, or that they just plain don't believe in keeping the "poor" Aby inside. I gave a lecture a while ago, and I found some people very adamant about letting their cats run loose outside. I asked if they were aware of the dangers that could befall their pet. When I had finished speaking to them, they had changed their minds.

Even if there is actually a lot of land, there has to be a road nearby, and by chasing a leaf, a mouse, or a bird into the street, the pet could be killed by a car or a truck. It could be badly mutilated or killed by being caught in a trap. It could be attacked by a pack of dogs, get fleas, ear mites, and animal or insect bites. It could be poisoned, intentionally or not. It could be badly hurt in fights with other cats. It could eat a leukemic mouse and get leukemia. It could be scared by something and run away. But, most of all, due to the Aby's exquisite beauty, it might well be stolen. If you love your Abyssinian, as I love all of mine, you will never let it outside unless you are taking it somewhere in a safe carrier. Abys, like other cats, are domestic pets. They like to be inside where it is safe and warm.

Abys are "people cats"; they prefer to be with people at all times, not outside alone.

All of my Abys love to stretch out in the sun on their window perches, and in the summer they watch the birds and children at play and watch the clouds; they watch the blowing leaves in the fall and the snow in the winter, and I know, when I hear the screech of brakes, that all my Abys are safe. They are content, happy, and have never even tried to get out. I guess they are smart enough to know when they are well off! I feel that if you are lucky enough to have a beautiful Aby, you should be willing to care for it and keep it safe indoors.

Be very careful to prevent small kittens from falling from high places. Abys are quite fearless and have to be watched until they are big enough to handle high places. Even a short fall can cause damage or even death if the kitten lands the wrong way.

Since so many things can happen, you just have to do your best. Keep your Aby safe indoors and it will be your happy, purring companion for many years to come.

Opposite: Ming-Tai's Rufus, three-month-old ruddy male Aby bred by Ruth Cooke-Zimmermann and owned by Sheila Warmack. *Below:* Blue Somali. Always be sure your pet's toys are safe.

Breeding Your Abyssinian

If you have a beautiful female Abyssinian show cat of excellent breeder quality, that is registered and has a very good pedigree, and you plan to let her have a family, you will want the very best stud cat to complement her beauty. If you bought her intending to breed her when she is of age, you should start looking around for a super stud for her long before you will need him. When it is time for her to be bred, usually around one year of age, it is a little late to try to locate the best male possible. You will want a stud that will complement your female in style, body type, color, and temperament. If she is lacking in any of these qualities or needs a bit of improvement, look for a male strong in her weakest points. Don't use just any male because he happens to be available. He might introduce dark roots, lack of color, necklaces or leg bars, or bad disposition into your lines and you would just be going backwards, because then you would have to try to breed these problems out in your next few breedings. It's better to let her skip a mating and then try for the best male you can find. As breeders, we are all dedicated to improving the breed; therefore, we are very selective in the studs we use.

I have what is called a "closed cattery," which means that I have my own studs that are used only by my own females; and I never send out any of my females to be bred elsewhere. I have eight different lines for this purpose. This has worked out very well, both for me and for my Abyssinians, toward preventing unwanted illness either brought back by my females from another cattery or brought into my cattery by visiting females. It also keeps away fleas, ear mites and fungus. Many breeders who want to use my studs get upset with me when I refuse them, but when I explain why my cattery is closed, they understand.

A female in season taken to or shipped to a strange male will be frightened of new surroundings, people, smells, and cats. She may go right out of season, especially if this is her first "experience." You can either bring her back home unmated or leave her with the stud's owners until she has her next season. However, she will be unhappy without you and may not go back into season while she is away. Having my own stud cats, I don't encounter this problem. My Abys are used to each other, and when it is time to breed a female, my males are right here and more than willing to oblige.

Opposite: Profile of a lovely show-quality Abyssinian owned by Linda B. Jones.

When the male and female mate, the male mounts the female from behind and with his teeth grabs her by the back of her neck to hold her steady. When a new male is studding for the first time, he soon learns not to hurt the female's neck or he will be swatted by his new "love." The female raises her back end and treads with her hind feet. At the moment of mating, the female lets out a shrill cry.

I pick up the male quickly and return him to his cage as soon as the mating is completed, because it is normal for the female to lash out at the male at this time, hissing and spitting and trying to attack him. A male could thus be badly hurt, but

Mating of two red Abys, DblCh. Ming-Tai's Flaming Pharos (male) and Absalon's Red Flame of Ming-Tai (female). Owner, Ruth Cooke-Zimmermann; breeder of female, Beverly Karole.

Ming-Tai's Eddie (bred by Ruth Cooke-Zimmermann and owned by Dawn Grubb) with Chili the dog. Both the male and the female prospective parents must be in excellent physical condition before the mating takes place.

most instinctively rear back to protect themselves. However, my cats, being the virile darlings they are, try to catch the female to mate again, even when she is in this most unpleasant mood, and they must be restrained.

After the mating, the female then goes into a frenzy of rolling and thrashing around that can appear quite violent. This rolling is necessary for a successful mating, since this is when the female releases her eggs to be fertilized. If your Aby female just sits there calmly after being mated, chances are the mating wasn't a success. Wait a few hours and try again, but if she consistently stays calm and doesn't get pregnant, she may be sterile. Have a talk with your

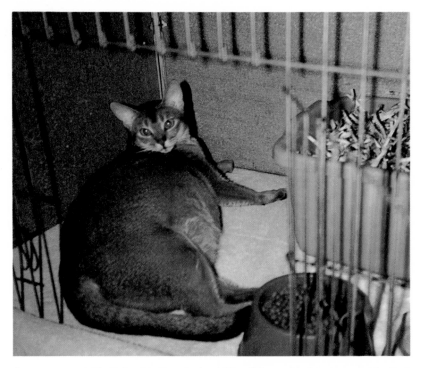

A very pregnant Ch. Bojangles Foxy Lady of Ming-Tai, a ruddy female owned by Ruth Cooke-Zimmermann and bred by Meredith Roberts. The impending litter was sired by Ming-Tai's Flaming Pharos, bred and owned by Ruth Cooke-Zimmermann. She had six kittens, a big litter for an Aby.

vet about it. Unfortunately, dogs can be artificially inseminated, but cats cannot.

I put my mating "lovers" together four or five times a day for as many days as they still want to mate. This may be any time from one day to a week. Then they will just ignore each other when her season has ended. If you leave them together all the time, they can quickly become worn out by constant matings. Most vets say that two matings within 24 hours are sufficient.

Most females cease calling when they stop mating, but others will call for a few days more, even though they will no longer accept the advances of the male.

Before you breed your female, make sure she has had her latest booster shot to give her babies the most protection they can get. In addition have her checked for worms so she won't pass them on to her kittens.

It is most important to clip her nails so that if she does catch the male when she lashes out at him, she won't hurt him as badly. This is especially important if it is her first mating and she is frightened.

If breeding is new to you, get a good book on the subject and read up on it first. Breeding Abys can be a nervewracking, difficult, worrisome, sometimes heartbreaking choice, and you want to be quite sure before you start. Most Abyssinians are very good mothers, but the new kittens are big, have big heads, and deliveries are usually hard. I was used to my Siamese females having eight squealing babies in an hour, but this is not the case in Aby deliveries. I hand-deliver every kitten and I stay with my pregnant females from a few days to two weeks before they are due, until they have safely had their new families and are calmly settled down with them.

I was warned in the very beginning that breeding Abyssinians would be a challenge, and, believe me, it surely has been and still is. But when the new little family is complete, I look at the happy mother with her paw around her chinchilla-soft, beautiful babies, and I know that it was all worth it!

Unless you can be with your female when she delivers, don't breed her. If she has her kittens alone, especially a first litter, you could lose both your Aby and her kittens if an emergency occurs during the birth. The old advice of putting the cat in a box in the back of a dark closet alone to deliver could be a disaster. If you love her, you will be there to calm her, help her if she needs it, and to give her moral support!!

CARE OF THE PREGNANT ABY

If you have mated your female Aby, the first sign of pregnancy is usually when her nipples become slightly enlarged and pink at about three weeks into the pregnancy. Most of my newly pregnant cats, as well as those belonging to my friends, have morning sickness for a few weeks. If mine start to spit up a bit each morning, I can be pretty sure they are pregnant. Aby pregnancies usually last between 65 to 68 days—some a few days less and some slightly longer. They start to show a slight bulge in the sides midway through their pregnancy. I don't change their diet except to switch to the special food for pregnant and nursing mothers. If they want more food as they progress in their pregnancy, I give it to them. When they show signs of being due, I give them evaporated milk and continue it for a few days after delivery unless it causes loose bowels.

A pregnant Aby should be confined to an area in which it can't jump. Jumping by a heavily pregnant Aby could endanger both mother and kits.

A box big enough for the mother to stretch out in should be ready two weeks before she is due. I cut down the center of the box half way in the front and on one side to make it easier for her to enter and leave the box. The mother-to-be will probably sleep in this box, thus getting used to it. Be sure it is in a warm spot where you can watch her.

Put a layer of clean newspapers in the bottom of the box, and then put in several old soft towels. Put down only a few

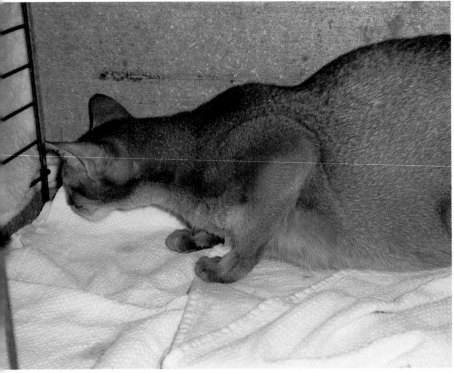

Absalon's Red Flame of Ming-Tai going into labor. Owner, Ruth Cooke-Zimmermann.

Gr. Ch. Purssynian's Faux Paw, an eight-week-old ruddy Aby kitten. Bred and owned by Beth and Darrell Newkirk.

at first until she is really in labor, because it is normal, as labor approaches, for the female to rip and tear up the contents of her box to make a nest. It's really a mess but a normal thing for her to do, and as many times as you try to straighten it, she will rip it up all over again.

A week before the due date, I assemble my "birthing kit." This consists of sterilized blunt-end scissors; iodine; white thread or dental floss; a pen; my birthing record book; paper towels; tissues; soft, clean washcloths; a clock or watch; a paper bag for rubbish; plenty of clean soft, old towels; and an electric room heater if the weather is cold.

If your pregnant Aby is a few days late, is eating well and is content, and she seems well and healthy, don't immediately rush her off to the vet for a C-section. She may not have conceived until the last day she was mated, making her due date later, depending on just how many days she was mated. If she does appear ill or uncomfortable, won't eat or drink water, or has a heavy discharge, a call to your vet is in order. You should notify him anyway that you are expecting a litter to make sure he is available if you do have an emergency. If he won't be there, he will tell you who will be covering for him, and that will save you time if you need help.

Most pregnant Abys will be quite restless and noisier than usual, pacing and crying, for a day or two before delivery. Your pet may start having a slight discharge, alerting you that the birth is near. (Call your vet if she is bleeding heavily.) Other pregnant Abys just seem to know when their time comes, and start to push.

The first litter is the hardest, since the Aby doesn't know what is happening and can be quite frightened. Comfort and

Basketful of kittens. As the kittens start to explore, their personalities will be come more and more distinct.

Four-week-old ruddy kittens bred and owned by Ruth Cooke-Zimmermann.

reassure her, and do all you can to keep her calm, talking softly to her and patting her. The delivering Aby may be terrified of the first kitten in her first litter, especially when it makes its first loud noises. Let her study her new baby while you are softly praising her. Nature should soon take its course and she will lick it and cuddle it to her. If she steadfastly refuses to accept her new family, or tries in her fright to hurt them, your vet will instruct you in the kittens' care and feeding. This can be a very time-consuming job, but it is most necessary if you want to save the litter.

Don't give up on this reluctant mother. Give her a chance to have another litter, and she will probably be a model mother. If she refuses her kittens again, you may decide not to breed this female again, and have her spayed. (Many women aren't cut out to be mothers, either!)

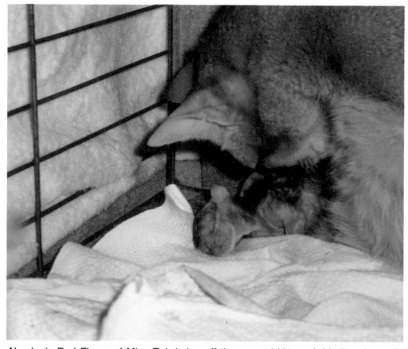

Absalon's Red Flame of Ming-Tai drying off the second kitten of this litter immediately after its birth. Owner, Ruth Cooke-Zimmermann.

If you have another nursing mother with a young litter, she could serve as a surrogate mother for you. Rub your hands through her hair and then rub each baby and put them to her nipples, and she will almost always lick them immediately and accept them as her own.

DELIVERY

When the female really starts her contractions, I slide out the shredded paper and put four layers of clean towels under her. If she is in a birthing cage, I then remove her food, water, and litter. This way, as the towels are soiled or wet I can slip out the top layer, leaving the cage or box always dry and clean for her.

As each kitten is born, you will see that, if the mother hasn't broken the bubble as soon as it appears, each is born in a sac of fluids. If the mother doesn't break this sac immediately, you must grasp it with your thumbnail and index fingernail under the kitten's chin, break it (it is very tough), and draw it back over the kitten's head so it can breathe. If you don't do this, the kitten could drown in the fluids. The new mother should lick her kittens vigorously to dry them off, stimulate their breathing, and get the blood flowing as it should.

After the afterbirth, or placenta, is expelled, the mother should break the umbilical cord with her teeth and will try to eat the afterbirth to get rid of it. Some just can't seem to do this, so dispose of it. My vet suggests letting the queen eat one if she insists and disposing of the others. There are varying opinions among vets as to the merits, or lack thereof, of eating these placentas. Follow your vet's advice.

If the Aby mother doesn't break the cord, tie it off tightly with thread, about two inches from the body, to prevent it from bleeding, and cut it with the sterilized scissors. Put a tiny drop of iodine on the cut end of the cord.

If the new mother doesn't lick the kitten dry, especially in cold weather, use one of your soft

Absalon's Red Flame of Ming-Tai's six-hour-old litter. Abyssinians have smaller litters than most breeds of cat. Owner, Ruth Cooke-Zimmermann.

Absalon's Red Flame of Ming-Tai and her brand new litter, sired by Ming-Tai's Flaming Pharos. Owner and breeder of litter and sire, Ruth Cooke-Zimmermann; breeder of dam, Beverly Karole.

washcloths or towels to rub the baby dry. I also hold each new kitten upside down and pat its back firmly several times to loosen any mucus that might be in the air passageways.

Some kittens are born only minutes apart, but usually the new mother can rest for a good 20 minutes before starting contractions for her next kitten. It may be that she will take a nice nap and have only one kitten per hour. This is easier on her but harder on you.

If the pregnant Aby has been in hard labor for three hours with no results, call your vet. A kitten could be in the wrong position. The longer the queen struggles, the weaker she will become. Without medical help, you could lose both the mother and her kittens.

As each kitten is born, I note the time in my birthing book. I also make a note of whether the birth was hard or easy, if it was frontal or breech, and how the mother behaved. When the litter is complete and the new family is resting, I write my overall view of the delivery; whether it was on time or late, whether the mother was nervous or calm, whether she cleaned up the kittens herself or not, how she accepted her new family, and anything that would be of help to me if I mate this same female again. I find that just about every female I have, if she is three days late, will always be three days late.

Make very sure a placenta is expelled after every kitten. If any are retained, they could cause an infection serious enough for you to lose your Aby. To prevent complications your vet can give her a shot within 24 hours to help her expel any tissue retained.

Since newborn kittens can die very quickly from a chill, keep the room at 80°F (27°C) during the birthing and for a week after the birth, because a kitten can wander away from the warmth of the mother's body and get a chill if it can't find its way back. Some kittens will cry, but since Abys are so quiet, some won't cry; they should be observed frequently so you can return them to their mother's side.

In Abyssinians, both frontal presentation (head first) and breech (tail end first) are normal.

Absalon's Red Flame caring for her six-hour-old litter. The majority of Aby females are excellent mothers. Owner, Ruth Cooke-Zimmermann.

Naturally, frontal is easier on the mother, the kitten, and you! If the sac has been broken either by the mother by licking or during birth, it will be a "dry" birth and more difficult for all. If it is a dry breech birth, you might have to help your Aby. If she has pushed very hard for quite a while and all you see is a bit of tail and maybe part of one or two legs, grasp them gently with one of your soft towels, and as the Aby pushes, ease the kitten gently, and soon it will pop out. Sometimes the mother can push a breech kitten out only as far as its neck in a dry birth; in order to save them both, you will have to help by using the soft towel in the same way—gently.

When the birth is complete and the happy mother and her new family are all resting from their ordeal, slip out any more soiled or wet towels to make sure they have a clean dry bed. Let your new Aby mother sleep, and when she awakens, offer her some milk and some baby beef for protein and strength. Abys love it and it is easy on the tummy. If she doesn't want milk, offer her a drink of water. I place the dish right beside her so that she won't have to get up and disturb her new kittens.

Most breeders say that a pregnant Aby won't eat on the day she will be delivering, so this is how they know it is time. That would never work with my Abys!

I have had Abys in the middle of a strong contraction come over to share my yogurt. Mine also eat some baby beef and drink water in the middle of the delivery. This is good because it gives them strength, but the majority of Abys don't do this.

Observe the new kittens to see if they are eating and are quiet and content. Feel their tummies to make sure they are fat and firm. If they are constantly fretting and crying, going from one nipple to another, and do not have firm tummies, your Aby may have no milk and a call to your vet is in order.

For the first two to three weeks of your new kittens' lives, they will just eat and sleep, growing rapidly every day. Some time during the second week their eyes will open. If an eye should stick closed, bathe it gently with clean cotton and warm water. If it continues to stick, your vet can give you a salve to use in case of infection. Don't delay, but call him as soon as this happens. The sooner it is treated the more quickly it will clear up.

Between the third and fourth week, the kittens will climb out of their nesting box into the new world. Make sure they are in a warm area where they can't get stepped on. I usually put my new kittens, with their mother, into a six-foot kitten cage for their own protection. This prevents them

Five-day-old litter, which consists of three blues and two fawns. Breeders/owners, Beth and Darrell Newkirk.

from being stepped on and from picking up germs brought in on our shoes, and it keeps them warmer than the floor. It makes the mother Aby happier, too. As soon as the kittens leave their nesting box and have their sea legs under them, I offer them mild cat food, usually a chicken dinner type, and a small dish of water.

The kittens are ready to go to their new homes between three and four months of age. Many people want tiny kittens of six or seven weeks of age, and I have seen ads in the paper for very young Abys. All kittens should have a full eight weeks to nurse from their mother for the best results for both the mother and the kittens. They should not go to their new homes until they have been properly immunized, are eating well, and are using the litter box. They should be playful, outgoing, and friendly.

Traveling with Your Aby

Most Abys are very good travelers. If they are show cats, they are well used to traveling to and from shows. The most important thing is to never take your cat or kitten anywhere without the protection of a cat carrier. These come in all types and all sizes, so when your Aby kitten is very small and you go to buy a carrier, remember that the kitten will grow very rapidly, and since carriers do tend to be quite expensive, plan ahead and buy a good-sized one.

Depending on the weather in your area, you should decide if you want an open or closed type. I have both the airline type and the plastic-domed ones, small, medium, and large. In the cold winter weather I use the closed ones, and when the weather is hot, I use the airline type with the

Somali kitten owned by Gale Taylor. If you don't want to share your bed with your new pet, start training him, at a young age, to sleep in his own bed.

Blue Aby kitten owned by Dean Mastrangelo. It is a good idea to bring along some of your pet's favorite toys when you travel with him.

wire door. Whichever I use, I have made "foul weather" clear plastic covers to keep out the freezing winds, rain or snow while I am between the car and the house or building I am going to. I remove the covers once we get inside. You will always need a carrier for your vet visits, so it is best to get your Aby acquainted with it right away.

Many owners buy or make heavy quilted covers for their carriers for the bad weather, but this way the Aby can't see out, and since Abys are born inquisitive, the clear plastic is much better.

Motels and hotels use strong chemicals both in the bathrooms and on the rugs, so I always bring the biggest size airline type carrier if we have to stay overnight in a motel or hotel; this way I know my Abys will be safe.

My big carriers are large enough for a small litter box, food, water, and a soft towel to sleep on. If the trip is long, I also use the big carriers in the car. It is much safer to have the Aby use the litter box in the carrier than to remove the cat from a small carrier and run the risk of its getting away from you and hiding under the car seat, or escaping if the door or window has to be opened to pay a toll. Always use a carrier to protect both your Aby and yourself.

A loose Aby in a motel room may hide when you are out to dinner, and if a cleaning crew opens the door, out it could go. Additionally, while they are cleaning your room, they may open the windows or terrace doors and then turn on a noisy vacuum cleaner, causing the already frightened Aby to run for its life. If the room is on an upper floor, that's the end of your Aby! Finally, people can tell by the beauty of an Abyssinian that it is a valuable cat, and it could very well be stolen.

When we have to travel, we bring a big cooler of food so we can eat without leaving our cats, but if it is necessary to leave the room for a short while, I have small locks that I put on each big carrier. I also have my cattery name in very large, fluorescent letters on each carrier, on both sides and the front, so it can be easily spotted if stolen.

Another important thing to remember is that most motel rooms are kept much colder than you would keep your home. Bring blankets or large, heavy beach towels to wrap around your carriers, leaving a space for your Aby to see you and to breathe, and fasten the covering with wooden clothespins so your Aby won't push it off and be cold while you sleep. With the cover in place, the cat's body heat will stay in and keep it warm.

If you have an Aby that gets car sick, feed a light meal early the night before the trip, and before you go to bed remove any food that isn't eaten. Don't feed the unhappy traveler in the morning, but wait to feed it after you reach your destination and it has settled down. If it is a long trip, try giving a small portion of strained baby beef in the middle of the trip, or at noon. Also offer a few licks of water if the Aby wants it. It is best to keep a small box of litter or a supply of newspaper and towels in the carrier in case of "thruway diarrhea," which many cats do get while traveling. It also helps to bring a plastic bag to keep the soiled towels in.

Many Abys outgrow carsickness, but some do not. One male I was showing would start to drool in the house as soon as I put him into his carrier, so the car had nothing to do with it. As soon as he reached the show hall, he always made a miraculous recovery and won every award there was!

I've seen many cats at shows so "out of it" from tranquilizers that they sleep instead of showing their beauty well. An Aby that is too doped up to pose and prance won't be a winner and should have stayed at home.

If you plan a vacation and can't take your Aby with you, try to have a friend, relative, or neighbor come in a couple of times a day to feed, change litter,

Ruddy and blue Abys owned by Sheila Dentico. Whether you plan to take your pets to shows or on family vacations, be sure to purchase a proper carrier. Never let your pet ride loose in any type of vehicle.

Above: *Ch. Purssynian's Pink Floyd of Ming-Tai, fawn male, with a pal. Having your pet cared for at home while you're away rather than in a strange kennel will be much less stressful for your pet. Breeders, Beth and Darrell Newkirk; owner, Ruth Cooke-Zimmermann.* **Opposite:** *Lovely Aby owned by Linda B. Jones.*

and play with your Aby. The cat will be much happier in its own surroundings instead of being boarded in a strange place with barking dogs and cold runs. It will almost always pick up fleas, have food it doesn't like, and can develop airborne illnesses. Home care will keep your Aby much happier and keep you from worrying about it.

Showing Your Aby

If you have bought a beautiful well-bred Abyssinian as a breeder or show cat, and it looks to you like a real show winner, there are things you should do—if this is your first show cat—before whisking it off to a show.

First, you should send for a copy of both the show standards and the show rules of the association of your choice. Study them well, especially the Abyssinian standard, and look at your kitten or cat with a fair eye to see if it meets the standard. If you really think it does, visit a show or two, and observe the Abyssinian judgings to see how the cats being judged compare with your Aby. Try to find out just what the judges are looking for when they judge an Aby. Try to talk to Aby breeders if they aren't in a ring or busy with their cats,

Profile of a fawn Aby owned by Diane Jackson. Fawns are now accepted for showing in most cat associations.

Ming-Tai's Blazing Saddles, a ruddy male kitten bred and owned by Ruth Cooke-Zimmermann, in his cage at his first show. The ribbons on the front of the cage indicate all his final wins for the day.

and observe their cats in the benching area.

If you are still sure you have a winner, look up the shows in a cat publication, send a postcard to the entry clerk listed, and request a show flier and an entry blank for the show. If you have studied your show rules, you will know that the kitten class is from four months to eight months. At eight months the Aby becomes eligible to be shown in the Championship class. Neutered Abys are shown in the Alter class. Adult classes are usually:

Novice (sometimes Open)
Champion
Grand Champion
Master Grand (in some Associations)
Multiple Grand (in some Associations).

Your show rules will tell you how

If you plan to exhibit your pet or pets, accustom them, starting at a young age, to being handled by different people so they will know what to expect in the ring.

a Novice or Open becomes a Champion, and how a Champion becomes a Grand Champion.

Read the show flier thoroughly when you receive it, and follow the instructions for entering the show. You must print or type clearly on your entry form all the information asked for in the flier. Be sure you enter well before the closing date that appears on the

flier; this is the date when they stop taking entries, and, if it happens to be a very popular show, it could be filled well before the date on the flier. Therefore, enter early to be sure you'll be accepted.

I will tell you now that showing is exhilarating, frustrating, nerve-wracking, satisfying, exhausting, expensive, thrilling, and depressing all at the same time. You can have the top cat and win everything in one ring, be on cloud nine, and in the next ring do absolutely nothing. You need nerves of iron, believe me! Every judge sees each cat differently, so be a good loser as well as a good winner. As well as nerves of steel, you will need the patience of a saint! If you have a good Abyssinian, the competition is usually fierce, and the tension can be just about unbearable. I know, because I've been there many times! If you think you can stand it, good luck, because no matter how many

years you show, the competition and tension get worse. Just when you think you have a clear shot at Grand Champion, along comes a gorgeous new cat that wipes every other cat out of its path.

The cage size is usually stated in the flier. You will need a large piece of material, in a color complementary to your Aby, to make drapes for your assigned benching cage. Use colorful plastic clothespins to anchor the drapes in place. You will also need a rug or heavy towel to cover the cage floor.

When you check into the show

Abyssinians snapped at a moment of repose at a show. Note the colorful cage curtains in the background.

hall the morning of the show, you will receive a card with your cat's name and number on it and be given directions to your assigned benching cage. This is where you keep your cat between judgings. When his number is called over the loudspeaker, carry him to the announced ring to be judged. You really have to listen intently in a noisy hall, because if you don't hear your number, you are given three calls, after which your cat is marked absent in that ring. You don't want to miss a single ring, so pay strict attention to the numbers as they are called out. In the show catalogue there will be a schedule for the day, so you will know just about when your cat will be judged by checking which breed is being judged at what time. Catalogues may be bought on your way into the show hall when you check in. All the cats are listed by number, breed, and name, with a space for you to enter any wins they might get; the blank final pages are in the back.

You will need an inexpensive suitcase in which to carry your show supplies. First, you need paper towels and a safe antiseptic to clean out the cage and dry it before hanging the drapes. If your cat has never been caged, put it in a cage or a large carrier several times a day for a week or two before the show to let him become accustomed to being confined so he won't be too scared at the show. He will have enough to get used to as it is. Stand your Aby on a table every day and try to do what you have seen the judges do so your Aby will get used to it.

In your show suitcase, you will need small weighted water dishes for every cat you bring and a thermos of water, from home, to prevent tummy upsets and long walks to the water fountain. To prevent spills, remove the water as soon as your Aby has had a good drink. Never leave your Abys unattended for a minute, since sad things have happened to Abys and other cats at shows when "sick" people decide to either steal your beauty or eliminate it from competition with poison. I don't like to mention this, but unfortunately it has become very prevalent.

Bring your Aby's favorite food, a can opener if you need it, a spoon, and small paper dishes to feed it. (You'd be surprised at how many long-time show people still always forget a can opener!) Cat food is usually supplied at shows, but if it isn't what your Aby is used to, use your own. Also bring a favorite toy and a sheet of clear plastic to cover the cage if it is drafty and cold in the hall. You can fold it on top of your cage and drop it down the front if it is needed.

We have a folding grooming

A young blue Somali

table that fastens onto the front of the cage. It is most handy for writing, eating, playing cards, or even taking a quick snooze.

Make very sure that your cage materials and rugs and all the clothes you wear in the show hall are completely washable, as they should be washed as soon as you get home from the show.

This will prevent any airborne germs picked up at the show from infecting your other cats, especially kittens, at home. Keep the carriers you used in the hall away from your other cats until they can be well washed and aired out in the sun for a day.

All cats being shown should be clean and free of fleas or ear

Dearabi Adagio of Jocar, a fawn Aby bred and owned by Cornelia Tichenor. Keep in mind that the true beauty of a show-quality Abyssinian takes months to develop—a growing kitten's appearance will seem to change every day.

Gr. Ch. Jeannel Charlie, bred and owned by Donna Jean Thompson.

mites. I bathe mine two days before the show, using a feline protein shampoo (available at pet shops) and rinsing them squeaky clean. Make sure all claws, front and back, are trimmed to protect the judge as well as yourself.

Now you are all set to go to the show. As soon as you get settled, make a note of your Aby's number (I write it on the

Before entering your pet in its first show, do your homework! Study the standard and get an idea of what a show-winning cat looks like.

front of my catalogue), listen well for your call to go to the judging ring, and hope for the best.

You should never talk to a judge until the end of the day, when the finals are over. If you have to speak to anyone about your cat, the only one you can talk to is the clerk seated at the judge's table. This is a very strict rule.

We should discuss what you should bring to a show for yourself. If it is your first show, bring your show rules and standards to refer to, but after a few shows you will be a pro and won't need them.

Most importantly, remember that a cat show is not a fashion show! Dress comfortably! Wear comfortable shoes, not four-inch spikes, as you will be doing a lot of walking to and from the rings, as well as a lot of standing. Bring a lunch, snacks, yogurt, sandwiches—enough to last all day—and a big thermos of your favorite non-alcoholic beverage. People food is usually for sale at every show.

Bring a sweater or light jacket in case the show hall is drafty. Most are well heated, ventilated or air-conditioned, but occasionally we run into a very hot or cold hall.

Any medicines you must take should be brought with you, and a very good headache remedy is a must!! There is no place like a cat show to get a splitting headache—super-tension, smoke-filled air, lack of sleep, a long ride—but how great it is to see your beautiful Aby with Best In Show. That's the name of the game, and then you know it was all worth it!

Be gracious if you win and be

If you should be lucky enough to have a show-winning Aby, be a gracious winner. Don't look a gift cat in the mouth.

The regal beauty of the Abyssinian makes this breed a perennial favorite at cat shows around the world.

gracious if you don't. Not every cat can be a winner since many shows have between 200 and 300 cats being judged, and most judges try very hard to be fair. It is a very hard job to pick five or ten top cats for finals out of all of those beautiful show cats, so if you win, you should be very proud of your Abyssinian. The judges are damned if they do and damned if they don't. They get scratched, clawed, bitten, hissed at, sprayed on, and abused by many cat owners, but they remain cat lovers and cat judges. They deserve a medal. You'll love to win, but be a good loser, too. If you carry on at a show, badmouthing the winners and the judges in a nice loud voice, you will be heard all right, and people will remember you! Keeping calm and quiet is best for your cat and for your own image, especially if you are new to the show scene. Good luck!!

Record Keeping

If you have one Abyssinian or a houseful, you should keep accurate records from the time each cat is born. I have a loose-leaf notebook indexed for each Aby. In each cat's section I have the Aby's name, birth date, sire and dam, and registration numbers as a heading. All immunizations are listed by date: what was given and by whom.

Leukemia testing dates are recorded by date and results noted, as are worm tests and their results. This way I know just by checking my notebook when each booster shot is due. I also make a note if a cat has a reaction to any shot or food, and I record any special vet visits, what they were for, any medicine prescribed, and the dates.

Ch. Purssynian's Pink Floyd of Ming-Tai, fawn male Aby bred by Beth and Darrell Newkirk and owned by Ruth Cooke-Zimmermann.

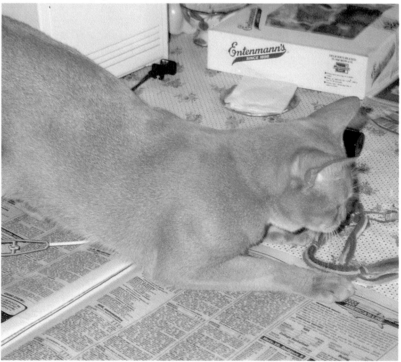

It is most important to keep a birthing record. This is very valuable for review, as the next time each female is mated you will know in advance what to expect. Of course, keep in mind that no two deliveries are the same, even with the same cat, but individuals do seem to follow a pattern.

A quick reference before breeding and again before delivery can be a big help to you. Although most Abys are frightened with their first litter,

Whether or not you plan to become a serious breeder and show person, you should begin to keep accurate records for each of your cats as soon as they come into your home.

they are much more settled during subsequent birthings. You will note which Abys, if any, refused their litter; this knowledge can help you to decide if you want to try again.

If you are a breeder, you will need a cattery receipt book to give each kitten buyer a complete receipt at time of purchase. These forms state whether registration papers are given, whether the kitten was sold with a spay or neuter agreement, birth date, sire and dam, and health guarantee, as well as the name, address, and phone number of the buyer. Be sure each receipt is in duplicate—one copy for the buyer and one for your records.

Each Aby should have a file folder or large envelope for its registration papers, pedigree, champion or grand champion records (lucky you!), and any important information pertaining to each cat. Keep all of these together in a safe place.

I have a metal file with folders for each cat, association and breed club information, dues cards, magazine renewal dates, and all important papers such as show rules and standards, show entry forms, litter registration forms, and correspondence concerning my cats or cattery.

I also keep a show record book, complete with name of show, the club sponsoring the show, date, and where it was

The better the records you keep about a particular cat, the more likely you will be to correctly predict the quality of its progeny.

held. I note the condition of the show hall and rest rooms; the proximity of parking; if there were a lot of stairs to climb to the show hall; if the show hall was well ventilated, heated or air-conditioned; and if the aisles were wide enough to permit walking to and from the rings safely. I record whether the lighting was adequate, allowing our Abyssinians to look like the colorful cats they are or like beige "nothings" due to the pink or blue lights in most gyms. I also list the name of each judge and the wins each cat had or didn't have including finals. I note mileage to and from the show hall, and whether it is a two-day show. I also like to include a note of the accommodations and restaurants. This way I have a handy record of which shows I will return to in the future.

Summation

I have tried to update my first Aby book, *Abyssinians,* by writing about the new body types of Aby, the new colors, new vaccines available to fight the Aby's most dreaded diseases, new foods available, and I have included the beautiful longhaired Aby, the Somali. I have tried to prove that if you want a loving, intelligent, alert, exquisitely beautiful, undemanding, quiet, loyal cat, an Abyssinian is for you! Abys have a unique way of wrapping themselves around your heart and filling your days with happy companionship and love. They ask nothing in return but lots of affection and good care. Among cats, Abyssinians are definitely "The Cream of the Crop"!!!

Below: Ming-Tai's Rockets Red Glare, three-month-old male (bred and owned by Ruth Cooke-Zimmermann), shadowboxing. *Opposite:* The Abyssinian is the perfect pet for anyone who wants a beautiful, loyal, affectionate yet undemanding cat. Once you choose an Aby, you will never be satisfied with anything else.

Suggested Reading

ATLAS OF CATS OF THE WORLD
By Dennis Kelsey-Wood
ISBN 0-86622-666-2
TFH TS-127

Contents: Natural History, The History of Cats, Domestication, The Mind of the Cat, Functional Anatomy, Purchasing a Cat, Nutrition, General Care, Practical Breeding, Breeding Theory, Exhibition, Health Care, The Domestic Cat Breeds, Coat Color in Cats, Cat Registration Bodies, Exporting Cats.

Audience: This comprehensive volume contains everything the cat lover needs to know. The detailed information on genetics appeals to the experienced fancier whose interest lies in breeding, while practical, "no-nonsense" guidelines help the beginner choose the right cat. Emphasis is placed upon good maintenance and the understanding of the cat's psychology and anatomy. The color photos and illustrations of every established cat breed (and many experimental varieties) as well as descriptions and depictions of wild species make this book a must for all feline fanciers.

ENCYCLOPEDIA OF AMERICAN CAT BREEDS
By Meredith Wilson
ISBN 0-87666-855-4
TFH H-997

Contents: The Breeds— Abyssinian, American Shorthair, American Wirehair, Balinese, Birman, Bombay, British Shorthair, Burmese, Chartreux, Colorpoint Shorthair, Egyptian Mau, Exotic Shorthair, Havana Brown, Himalayan, Japanese Bobtail, Korat, Maine Coon, Manx, Manx Longhair, Oriental Shorthair, Persian, Ragdoll, Rex, Russian Blue, Scottish Fold, Siamese, Somali, Sphynx, Tonkinese, Turkish Angora. Color Standards—Abyssinian, Somali, Burmese, Cameos, Egyptian Mau, Japanese Bobtail, Particolors, Pointed Cats, Silver Smokes, Solid Colors, Tabby, Tonkinese.

Audience: An authoritative book that covers the American and Canadian breeds and illustrates them by using strictly American and Canadian cats. A highly colorful book that is a must for cat lovers and cat breeders.

Index

ABYSSINIANS
KW-223